Proposal Writing For Smaller Businesses

Who Want To Become Bigger Businesses!

I0470358

Proposal Writing For Smaller Businesses
Who Want To Become Bigger Businesses!

Lee Lister is a Business Consultant with more than 25 year's consultancy experience for many household names. She is known as The Bid Manager or The Biz Guru.

From an early age she began an unparalleled journey through business consulting that continues to span across the UK, USA, Europe and Asia. She has consulted for many companies all over the world. Specialising in business change management, start up consultancy and trouble shooting. She is highly skilled in seminars, lectures and corporate presentations on business, project management and bid management. Lee's experience in marketing and internet marketing is also keenly sought after.

She is a prolific published writer of books, ebooks and articles on business, entrepreneurship and bid management. She can easily be found on major search engines and Amazon.

Proposal Writing For Smaller Businesses
Who Want To Become Bigger Businesses!

First published in Great Britain in 2009.

Publisher: Biz Guru Ltd

ISBN: 978-0-9563861-0-6

This book is dedicated to my daughter Kerry Lister for whom I have always strived to be my best.

Other books available include:

FastTrack© Bid Management

FastTrack© The Winning Solution

FastTrack© Project Management

FastTrack© To Job Success

Entrepreneur's Apprentice

How Much Does It Cost To Start A New Business?

Start My New Cake Decorating Business

Start My New T Shirt Decorating Business

Proposal Writing For Smaller Businesses

Who Want To Become Bigger Businesses!

Author: Lee Lister

www.Bid-Manager.com

www.StartMyNewBusiness.com

Proposal Writing For Smaller Businesses

Who Want To Become Bigger Businesses!

Contents

Legal Notice

We do not believe in get rich quick schemes. We do believe that business is equal parts of inspiration, hard work and luck. We ensure that every book that we sell will be interesting and useful to our clients. Every effort has been made to accurately represent our product and it's potential. Any testimonials and examples used are not intended to represent the average purchaser and are not intended to guarantee that anyone will achieve the same or similar results

Please remember that each individual's success depends on his or her background, dedication, desire, and motivation. As with any business endeavour, there is an inherent risk of loss of capital. **There is no guarantee that you will earn any money**.

This book will provide you with a number of suggestions you can use to better guarantee your chances for success. **We do not and cannot guarantee any level of profits.**

This product is written with the warning that any and every business venture contains risks, and any number of alternatives. We do not suggest that any one way is the right way or that our suggestions are the only way. On the contrary, we advise that before investing any money in a business venture you seek counselling and help from a qualified accountant and/or attorney.

> **You read and use this book on the strict understanding that you alone are responsible for the success or failure of your business decisions relating to any information presented by our company Biz Guru Ltd.**

Why Spend Time Writing Proposals?

Well the simple answer is that as your business gets bigger you will reach the stage where the easiest way to increase your business size is to bid (or tender/propose) for more business. So common is putting future work out for tender that it is hard to see how you can expand your business without learning how to write a winning proposal!

So what is in a winning proposal? Simply put, you are showing what solution you can provide to your potential customer, at what price and just as importantly, why your company is the best to provide this solution. Seems simple doesn't it? Well yes – except that your competitors will also be bidding against you. Add to this is the fact that a proposal is a legal document that may lead you into a whole lot of expensive trouble and you can see why you need to learn how to write winning proposals.

So let's look at what the proposal should do. Win of course, but before that you have to:

- Make your company stand out from the others as well as reflect the values and brand of your company.
- Offer the solution that is required in a format that is easily understood.
- Be well priced so as to attract the client, provide a profit for your company as well as opportunities for you both to work together in the future.
- Be well structured, well written and well presented.

So let's get started!

Preparing Your Company To Write Proposals

So you want to jump right into writing your proposals, but it is better to prepare your company first. Organisation preparation is vital so that you can:

- **Decide** what you do best and only chase the potential work that you have a good chance of winning.

- **Discover** which companies have potential projects that require your capabilities.

- **Sell** these capabilities to the companies in a way that makes you stand out from your competitors.

- **Minimise** the risk of undertaking the work so that you don't give away or lose all your profits.

- **Maximise** the return from your work and ensure that you are not throwing away your hard earned profits on lost causes.

Your preparation will consist of the following activities:

- **Reviewing** your existing resources.
- **Defining** your core capabilities.
- **Establishing** your potential.
- **Understand** your differences from your competitors.
- **Looking at** what partnerships you could make.
- **Establishing** your Costing Model.
- **Collating** together your standard documents.

Reviewing Your Existing Resources

Sit down with a cup of tea or coffee, a pen and paper and maybe a couple of trusted associates or employees and work out the answers to the following:

- What do you do best?
- What are you staff's key skills?
- What key resources do you have?
- Do you have any spare resources or staff time that you are not currently using?

- What spare capacity in equipment, down time or manufacturing time do you have?
- Can you easily, cheaply and quickly expand your product range or produce more of your existing products?
- Are some of your resources underutilised and can you think of something profitable and efficient to do with them?
- Can you quickly and profitably take on staff and resources to meet new business that you are chasing?
- Do you do something that your competitors do not do?
- What do you need to do to encourage your company to expand and can you easily obtain it?
- What can you do that which is totally "off the wall" or unexpected, but still uses your existing resources?
- Are some of your staff underutilised and can you think of something for them to do?

You should now have a list of your existing, or easily obtainable resources.

Defining Your Core Capabilities

So, what are you good at? What is the main thing that your company does? These are your core capabilities. When you start writing your proposals, it is important that you only write proposals for work that you can actually undertake and make a good profit. Sounds obvious, doesn't it? But in the heat of the excitement of proposal writing it is easy to exaggerate your potential. Take a few minutes to define your possible core capabilities. There is a table on the next page to help you.

Subject Area	Your Organisation's Capabilities
Products and/or Services	
Technical skills or experience	
Business skills or experience	
Project or team management	
Appropriate staff	
Support facilities	
Training Facilities	
Anything Else	

Establishing Your Potential

Similarly, you need to examine your existing capabilities and work out a natural progression of what you can potentially offer. Look at what you think that your organisation could do if it had the opportunity. For example look at:

- What would be a natural progression from your current work?
- Is there a complimentary service or product that you could offer?
- Is there a natural upgrade or extra that you could provide?
- Are there any goods or services that people ask you for that you don't currently have but you could profitably provide?
- What future products are your researching or developing, that you want to sell?
- What do you think that you can offer another company that they may need?
- What are you great at that your customers would like?
- Is there a hole in the market that you can fill?

- What do you think that other companies may require from you?
- Are you known for something that is sought after?
- Are there any markets would you like to develop or be more prominent in?
- What would you like your company to be remembered or renowned for?
- What can you can do to you make yourself stand out from your competitors?

Understand Your Differences

Now have a look at a few of your close competitors that you are likely to be bidding against.

- Do you know why you are the best company in your field and can you write down truthfully why?
- Do you know who your competitors are and what they do?
- What are your differentiators that set you apart from your competitors? That is, what do you do that is different and better that what they do.

- What is the best thing that you do?
- What are you renowned for and it the same as the best thing that you do?
- Do you have the only one of a kind product and can you change the product slightly to meet another market?
- Are you soon to bring something to market, or should you think about do this?

Answering all of the above questions should ensure that you understand what your company does best and hopefully better than your competitors. Taking some time to list your resources and core capabilities as this will be very useful when you start writing your proposals.

The Importance of Partnerships

It could be that when you start looking at potential work, that you decide that you are not big enough to bid. Don't worry about this – even the large blue chip companies work with other companies on bids.

Proposal Writing For Smaller Businesses
Who Want To Become Bigger Businesses!

You should look at working in partnership with other companies to not only make your company larger, but also to offer a better product portfolio to your potential customers. These companies can offer services that are complimentary to yours – e.g. plumbing and carpentry or fill in the services and products that you cannot.

Working with partners can bring you both benefits and problems. Some of he benefits of working with a partner are:

- Spread the risk and costs of bidding – preparing and writing proposals can be expensive.
- Obtain experiences that you do not have to make the bid that much more interesting and appropriate.
- Gaining corporate experience from each other.
- Your staff gain valuable skills and experience in larger projects than you currently undertake.

- Your organisation becomes better known within the market.
- The different views of life, problems and business that each of you have can be shared.

Your partner should also benefit! Please don't forget this if you want to repeat the process.

Of course there are going to be problems:
- You must get on and be able to work together on the resulting project. Arguments look unprofessional and cost money!
- You need clear boundaries and responsibilities and know who is in charge on the project. This may mean one company is in charge of the other's staff for some time.
- The split of work must be appropriate to reward – in other words – you receive the value of the work that you do.

- You need to check that you are not expected to be responsible for matters you have no control over?
- Your skills and experience must compliment each other so that you can help each other out as required.

So where do you find potential partners?

- They could be companies in a complimentary line of business.
- They could be in the same line of business as you, but like you are not quite big enough to bid on their own.
- They could be your subsidiary, or a different branch.

If there is a large ITT coming up, you should consider contacting another similar company of the same size as you and ask them to join forces with you in bidding for it. This will allow you both to compete for work that you would not normally be able to do.

Your Costing Model

Costing is very important; sometimes this is the "win or lose" activity. You should use a Costing Model to define and manage your costs during the proposal. In this way, you have a fair chance of winning and making a profit. Most companies use a spreadsheet based programme for calculations.

Your Costing Model should include:

- **All you cost elements.** As you produce your proposal make a note of all the costs that make up your bid. Include costs of borrowing money whilst you are waiting for your payments to be made.

- **Calculation of your costs.** You should use your Costing Model to calculate such costs as: your hourly costs by hourly rates, material costs by amount and processing costs by time.

- **Uplifts for profit**: Decide what percentage/amount you want to charge for project and do not forget to include costs or managing your sub contractors.

- **Uplifts for risk**: Decide how much each increment of risk you will be undertaking will increase your costs and include this. This is an area that many people forget.

- **Add extras**: Such as Taxes, Delivery, Insurance etc. This are best itemised separately in any proposal.

- **Adjust to win**: Use your understanding of your potential client to make the appropriate adjustments to that you so not price yourself out of the market.

Designing Your Costing Model

What does a Costing Model look like? Well, your Costing Model should include:

- **Staff costs** - usually calculated by daily rates.

- **Resource costs** – computers, materials travel, variable costs etc.

- **Overheads** - office space, utilities, office costs etc.

- **Estimated costs for risk** - usually a % uplift depending on how risky it is.
- **Estimated profits** – usually a %
- **Contingency** – for delays, changes, illness etc.

Your Costing Model should take into account any NPV calculations that are requested. Care should be taken to ensure that the correct level of detail is provided. The Risk Review (more about this later in the book) that you will undertake will produce risk costs that should also be built in.

You should be careful that you split out taxes e.g. VAT or Sales Tax and any delivery charges as specified in the ITT (Invitation To Tender). Sometimes proposals can be provided on a "time and material basis" – in which case you need to place a floor and ceiling on your costs and specify exactly what the "time and the materials" are.

Documents And Stuff You Need Every Time

Now we come to the stuff that you will need every time you bid. Get them together now and it will not only save time, but also ensure that you have a good structured proposal template. The stuff you will need will consist of a pile of standard documents that you either use in the bid or refer to again and again. They should include:

- Company brochures.
- Company description.
- Company details such as formal name, shares, turnover etc.
- Company published accounts.
- CV/Resume of key staff.
- Company ethos, core capabilities etc.
- Product details.
- Standard processes and methods.

In addition there will be a number of documents that are requested time after time. These will include:

- Your Quality Statement.
- Your Health and Safety Statement.
- Business Continuity Statement.
- Diversity Charter/Equal Opportunities Charter.
- Data Security Statement.
- Confidentiality Agreement.

Don't worry if you don't know what these are – we'll go through them in the next chapter. At the moment you just need to know to keep them in a safe place you can find when you want to write your bid.

The Standard Statements

As you write your proposals you will notice, particularly if you work in the government, education, medical business environments, that the same questions keep getting asked and the same statements required. In fact in some business areas, particularly IT, up to 60% of your bid is the same every time. Here are a few of the more common statements asked for.

Quality Statement.

This is a statement of how you manage quality within your business. Here is a typical statement.

Statement Of Quality

Business Goal

To get it right first time, every time and strive to exceed customer expectations whenever possible. Our business system will conform to the requirements of ISO 9001.

Business Principles

Quality derives from a staff commitment to service and excellence. This belief is stated as business principles:-

Customer Focus

Customer requirements come first. Quality begins and ends with the customer and we strive to always satisfy their needs. This is reflected in our flexibility - both as individuals and as an organisation.

Relationships

We build mutually beneficial relationships with customers and suppliers.

Innovation

We search for, design and supply creative products and services.

Teamwork

Our Employees work together as a team to satisfy our customers.

Process Emphasis

We focus our Employees on practical processes to ensure consistent results.

Continual Improvement

Through management review of our Business Management System we aim to continually improve business performance, processes, products and services.

Employee Development

Through active mentoring we create a culture where staff have the skills and are empowered to take responsibility for the results of their actions which contributes to the success of the Company.

Health and Safety Statement.

This is a statement of compliance with Health and Safety requirements (UK) and looks something like this.

Health & Safety Policy Statement (UK)

Our statement of general policy is to:

- provide adequate control of the health and safety risks arising from our work activities;
- consult with our employees on matters affecting their health and safety;
- provide and maintain safe vehicles and equipment;
- ensure safe handling and use of vehicle equipment, as well as substances hazardous to health;
- provide information, instruction and supervision for employees;
- ensure all employees are competent to do their tasks, and to give them adequate training;

- prevent accidents and cases of work-related ill health;
- maintain safe and healthy working conditions;
- review and revise this policy as necessary at regular intervals.

Other similar statements used by other companies are:

Health & Safety Policy Statement (All else)

Our goals are to:

- Prevent workplace incidents and injuries.
- Continually improve our health and safety performance.
- Foster a culture in which all employees, partners, contractors and sub consultants share this commitment to health and safety.
- Have the best safety performance as compared to similar companies.

Proposal Writing For Smaller Businesses
Who Want To Become Bigger Businesses!

We will:

- Always manage our operations in the safest manner, by recognizing and assessing hazards and applying effective controls.
- Make safe conduct a condition of employment.
- Always comply with health and safety legislation and guidelines.
- Ensure our managers and supervisors provide the tools, supervision, training and resources needed for our employees to work safely.
- Ensure our employees and others on our worksites work safely.
- Involve all employees in our health and safety management system through representation on joint health and safety committees.
- Review our health and safety performance regularly, evaluate performance information and communicate performance to all employees.

- Learn from our experiences to prevent future incidents.
- Ensure that our formalized health and safety management system remains current with industry best practices.

Diversity or Equal Opportunities Charter.

This is a statement that you understand about equal opportunities and what you intend to do to ensure that you do not stray from the ethos of the various Acts. Your Statement UK and USA should look something like this:

Equal Opportunities Policy Statement (UK)

Equal Opportunities involves both recognition and acceptance that discrimination and disadvantage lead some members of the community to be unjustifiably denied access to services and to employment. By adopting an Equal Opportunities XX seeks to redress this balance and ensure equal access to the services it provides and in its recruitment and employment practice.

XX is firmly committed to equal opportunities in every area of its work. We believe that we have much to learn and profit from diverse cultures and perspectives, and that such diversity will make our organisation more effective in providing a service to our customers.

XX is committed to developing and maintaining an organisation in which differing ideas, abilities, backgrounds and needs are fostered and valued, and where those with diverse backgrounds and experiences are able to participate and contribute.

XX recognises that Equal Opportunities is a part of the broad context of Good Practice in employment and service delivery. As such, principles of equality of opportunity are essential aspects of XX approach to the delivery of high quality services to its customers, both through its employees and its agents. Each XX employee or agent will, therefore, be expected to reflect these principles in every aspect of their dealings with co-workers and customers.

Discrimination and disadvantage have undermined the quality of life for many people. Eradication of such discrimination and disadvantage is a necessary way of improving the quality of life for all.

XX believes that: discrimination against any person or group is unjustifiable. XX is therefore keen to meet its obligations to promote equality of opportunity, required under the following legislation:

- Sex Discrimination Act 1975 (Amendment 2003)
- Race Relations Act 1976 (Amendment Act 2000)
- Race Relations Code of Practice (Approved by Parliament 1983
- Race Relations Act (Amendment 2003)
- Equal Pay Amendment Act 1984 (Amendment 2003)
- Disability Discrimination Act 1995
- Human Rights Act 1998
- Employment Equality (Religion or Belief)
- Employment Equality (Sexual Orientation)
- Employment Equality (Age discrimination)

Diversity Charter (US)

As a company we value people for their differences and actively promote diversity both within our internal business as well as our candidate and client base. This Diversity Charter outlines some of our working practices which, we hope, will assure you of a dedicated and professional team of experts working with you, whether you are seeking employment or employees through our company.

Our commitment to equality of opportunity for all, underpins all of our activities. One of our key objectives is to promote equal opportunities and reflect the diversity of our customers
and staff, throughout our services, sales, employment and training. We aim to deliver high-quality services to all of our customer in all of the communities we work in.

We strive to employ a diverse workforce, strengthened by the varied contribution of our staff.

We want to reflect the communities we work in, and aim to be an employer of choice in those areas.

Our vacancy advertisements are written in plain language and based upon the criteria required for the role, neither directly or indirectly discriminating against any candidates.

Our website provides a host of services for both candidates and clients. The site is accessibility compliant, accommodating those with sight disability.

Data Security Statement.

Data security is very important in the modern world and a Data Security Statement is often called for. It could look like this.

Data Security Statement

XX products and services meet the physical and technical standards, and provide all necessary controls for our customers to maintain their administrative security compliance standards.

Specifically, XX agrees to: Implement administrative, physical, and technical safeguards that reasonably and appropriately protect the confidentiality, integrity, and availability of the electronic protected financial information that it creates, receives, maintains, or transmits on behalf of our customers.

In summary, XX has implemented reasonable and appropriate safeguards to protect our customer's financial and business information. Furthermore, XX agrees to report to our customers any security incident of which it becomes aware, and will authorize the termination of any customer contract in the case of any material breach of this compliance statement.

Privacy Policy or Confidentiality Statement

This is a legal requirement in Europe and a suggestion for other countries. Here is the Privacy Policy of our company.

Privacy Policy of Biz Guru Ltd

Biz Guru is committed to protecting the privacy of the information we collect about you. We use the information we collect about you on this Site to provide a personalized service to you when you purchase goods and items from our sites and business.

What data do we collect?

So that we can provide a personalized service, upon the purchase of goods or services or at other times, we will ask you to submit your email address and you can also submit other optional personal information.

How is the information used?

Biz Guru will use the information you provide to us to identify your order, requests or comments and provide the appropriate services to you.

With whom is the information shared?

Biz Guru may disclose aggregate statistics about our Site visitors, customers and sales in order to describe our services to prospective partners, advertisers and other reputable third parties and for other lawful purposes, but these statistics will include no personally identifying information.

Biz Guru may disclose personal information if required to do so by law or if it believes that such action is necessary to protect and defend the rights, property or personal safety of Biz Guru , the Site or its visitors.

Our site contains links to other sites. Biz Guru is not responsible for the privacy policies or the content of such sites.

Security

Biz Guru places a great importance on the security of all personally identifiable information associated with our customers. We have security measures in place to attempt to protect against the loss, misuse and alteration of customer data under our control. While we cannot ensure or guarantee that loss, misuse or alteration of data will not occur, we use our best efforts to prevent this.

Where is the information stored

Information which you submit via the Site is sent to a computer located in England. This is necessary in order to process the information and to send you the information you have requested. Information submitted by you may be transferred by us to our other offices and to other reputable third party organizations, which may be situated outside the European Economic Area.

Your acceptance of the above uses of your personal data

By using this Site, you consent to the collection and use of this information by Biz Guru and to the Biz Guru privacy policy. If we change our privacy policy in any way, we will post these changes on this page but you are responsible for checking this policy each time you use the Site.

Your rights

You have a legal right to a copy of all the personal information about you held by us. You also have a right to correct any errors in that information. Regarding any questions, concerns or comments you have about this policy or the enforcement of your rights please email XX

Business Continuity

This is basically a statement of what you are going to do to keep the project going if something happens to your business to make it difficult to continue. This usually refers to Force Majeure. The document will look something like this:

Business Continuity Officer:

Contact Details:

Key Staff and Contact Details:

Alternative Office:

Actions on Disaster:

Staff:

Resources:

Project Activity:

Legal Notice

Lastly, you may need a Legal Notice – an example of which can be seen at the front of this book. Feel free to copy it or tailor it to your own needs.

Finding Your Opportunities

W ell, you are all set up – so now you need to find your opportunities. So where do you look?

- **Your existing clients** are the natural place to start. Your sales staff should be in regular contact with the companies that you have completed work with in the past. A reference from one part of the company so that you can also work in another part of the company is a great help. Try and set up the kind of relationship that ensures that you get to hear what is going to happen in a client's business in the future.

- **The internet** is another good place to look. There are numerous web sites where requests for proposals (ITT) and Invitation to Tender (ITT) are regularly listed. In addition government agencies also post their requirements. Set up a list of sites to regularly visit and get on their email alerts and mailing lists.

- **Regular bulletins** from periodicals, agencies, consultancies etc. can also be signed up for. Get yourself on mailing and email lists so that you get all the news about what is happening in your business world.

- **Trade publications** – get all the regular ones plus some niche ones if necessary and keep an eye on the adverts.

- **Professional contacts** – networking as always pays off. Spend some time each month networking, going to seminars and exhibitions and make contacts, get contact details, understand what other companies are doing etc.

Other places where ITT's come from are:

- A request made via your sales force.
- A request resulting from existing consulting.
- A direct request from the client.

Which only emphasises that you need to keep in contact with your current and past clients!

Should You Bid?

Sounds a silly question doesn't it? But before you chase all the opportunities you can find you need to remember that writing proposals takes time, money and effort. Not to forget that to keep on putting in great proposals and never winning does nothing for your self confidence.

You should be looking for a potential project that:

– Matches your abilities – can you actually do it with all your staff and resources?

– Has the potential to make a profit – after all your costs and efforts will you end up with a profit?

– Benefits your organisation – you need to keep your business expanding and growing so does this project stretch and/or improve your business and it's reputation within your business market place?

Next look as to whether you can actually do the project. Does the proposed project match your core capabilities?

- Can you do it within the time frame, with your resources and experience?
- Are your staff available when the project needs doing or will you have to take on extra staff and can you find them if you need to?
- Will your people be available for **the entire** project?
- Can you maintain the skills required?
- Do you have the time and resources available?
- Do you have support for what you are proposing?
- Will you be able to quickly set up the project and will it run smoothly?
- Will you benefit from the experience? No good completing a project if there is no profit or learning experience from it.

Next look at what the potential client is asking for. Are the client requirements?

- **Feasible** – that is can they be done? Many projects are not.

- **Technically possible?** Again many projects are not!

- **Worth the effort** – the cost of bidding means that you cannot chase every ITT. Bidding costs in time, effort and exposure are high and must be recouped from those bids you win.

- **Fit into your organisation profile** – you have spent money on your image and a group of products – to move out of this arena takes considerable thought and probably some great cost. Of course, sometimes organisations want to move away from their core business e.g. the move from hardware selling towards system integration.

- **Appropriate for your client?** Sometimes clients are their own worst enemies. No on will thank you for selling something that will not work and is not really what they want.

If all of the above criteria are met then you should go ahead with **considering** writing the proposal. You have one other thing to consider and it could be a big problem – Risk!

Risk

  - Has the potential to lose your profit
  - Causes problems in projects
  - Causes problems in professional relationships
  - COSTS MONEY

A risk is an event that is likely to cause an adverse impact to one or more of the following:

  - **Project budget** – what it is going to cost you to implement the winning solution.
  - **Project timeline** – how long it will REALLY take.
  - **Project deliverables** – what you have contracted to produce.
  - **Project resources** – what you will need to get to full implementation.

A risk is something is something that may happen – a good bid manager decides upon the likelihood of it happening and costs the proposal to take it into account. For this to be possible you need to look at your Risk Strategy.

Your Risk Strategy which will consist of:
- How much risk you will accept to win the bid.
- You risk increment costs.
- How much bid you pass down.
- How much risk cost uplift you manage.

It is defined after you decide upon:
- What level of risk is acceptable?
- What kinds of risks are acceptable?
- How do we cost the risks we accept?

There is a whole chapter identifying risks and explaining what to do with them later on in the book.

Payment Schedule

The last thing you need to look at before you decide whether to bid or not is the Payment Schedule. You need to check when you will be paid

- Is the first payment sufficient to cover up front costs?
- Is the payment flow fair and efficient?
- Are the conditions of payment fair?
- Will they be paid promptly?
- Will you need to borrow whilst the waiting for your money?

If all the above factors are fine then you can make your final decision as to whether you want to Bid or Not Bid.

Go/No Go Decision

The factors you should consider about whether to bid for a particular project are:

- What are the chances of success? It is rarely sensible to bid on work that you have little chance of winning.

- Possible profit Vs risks that you will undertake. Will it be worth it?
- Political or sales need to bid – sometimes you just need to bid to get into the company or remove another rival from the account regardless of whether you are going to make much of a profit.
- Are there other benefits of bidding? These could be such matters as being able to develop new products, trial new services or train new staff whilst earning on a project.

Lastly look at what happens if you do not bid?

- Will we lose face, status or be embarrassed?
- Will you lose the option to bid on further bids? Sometimes companies put out small projects with the potential to pick up more work in the future or become a "preferred supplier".
- Will you upset the client? Keeping current and potential clients happy is very important.

- Will you show your weaknesses and advertise to your competitors that you are not up to this kind of project?
- Will you show your strengths for little return if you undertake the project?

Bid and Cost Strategy

Now you know your risk and your rewards coming from potentially winning the bid. You have decided that you want to win. Now you need to decide your Bid and Cost Strategy – how do you want to approach and design the proposal?

- Bid high with quality
- Bid low with minimum compliance
- What level of compliance do you want to undertake. What do you think is the optimum mix of products and services that will meet the majority of the client's requirements?
- Extras – what other extras can you offer your potential client – maybe something that your competitors cannot?

- What to leave out – sometimes when trying to get to an optimum bid price – some of your offerings need to be stripped out.

So now you are ready to get writing?

Now You Need To Get Writing

All prepared? Got a suitable prospect and want to get going? Here we go then – the bit you have been waiting for – writing the proposal. If you have skipped the first few chapters then you really need to go back to them and read them – they are important and are going to save you a lot of time.

When you write a proposal there are a number of things that you have to do:

- Find out exactly what your potential client wants – not always what they ask for.
- Emphasise what you are best at in order to make your proposal stand out.
- Hide the bits where you are weakest. Obviously you need to be truthful in all you propose, but there is an art to ensuring that your weaknesses do not stand out too much.

What Do They Want?

Many ITT's have hidden agendas, some industries are probably worse than others. Have a look through the documents you receive and see if you can identify any of the following:

- **Political requirements** - Is there a political subtext?

- **Hidden agendas** – does a subject get mentioned more than once? If so make a note of it and make sure you can fulfil this wish.

- **Hobby horses** - does the funding body have a particular allegiance? Is there something that they have always wanted?

- **Shopping lists** – some ITT's ask for everything under the sun – try and ascertain what they are really after. Tread carefully when you complete these kinds of tenders. No one can fulfil all of these requirements but you have to manage expectations very carefully.

- **Missing items** – is what they are asking complete? Ensure that your potential customer has a working system when you have finished – they will be grateful.

Putting The Solution Together

Having established what your potential customer's requirements, you need to put together a solution that will solve their problems. In essence most projects seek to do one or more of the following:

- To improve the collection, collation, control and/or dispersion of information.
- To allow an organisation to make unique or innovative changes or progress (market advantage).
- To save manpower or other costs.
- To improve customer service.
- To solve a business problem that is causing delays, quality problems or extra costs.

You should now have a list of the problems that the potential customer is seeking to solve. Read the ITT through one more time and make a list of all the items, services, improvements, goods and process changes that they have asked for.

Now take this list – we will call it the Requirements List and against each item detail how your company (and partners) will solve these problems and deliver these requirements. By working from this Requirements List you should be able to come up with an overall solution. Of course, some ITT's will be simple, but it is a good habit to get into, so that as your business grows, you have learnt good bidding methods to help you. Remember that the solution you come up with should be:

- **Technically possible** by your existing services, goods, staff and available time.
- **Worth the effort.** No one wants to work hard for very little return.

- **Fit into your company profile.** Tempting as it may be to bid on new work, it is important that you don't step out of your comfort zone or let your company become known for services and goods that you cannot usually produce.

- **Appropriate for your client.** Your main outcome is for a profit for you and a successful business solution for your client. You want to walk away from a successful project leaving behind a happy client who will not only tell everyone how great you are, but will also want to work with you again.

When working out your solution you need to consider:

- **Technical solution** – how it will be done.
- **Project management** – what processes will be used and how will you manage the project, especially if your staff will be working off site.

- **Staffing** – who will do it and will people with the appropriate skills be available when they are needed.

- **Support** – how will the resulting work be supported and maintained during and after the project.

- **Other services available** – a good place for selling extra work.

- **Risks, problems and issues** – explain them to your client and how you will mitigate manage or avoid them.

- **Compliance** – you need to check which requirements you cannot meet and either not meet them or offer something of equal or better value.

Emphasising Your Best Bits

Now obviously you want to show off what you are best at. There are lots of ways to do this. When you look at a page, your eye is naturally drawn to the top left hand side – so this is where you put your best bits – the bits you do best.

Similarly when you get to the bottom right hand side of a page, that's when you remember what you have read in order to join it with the next page. This is where you put stuff you want to be remembered.

If you have a complex matter that needs to be explained to your potential client, then you should consider using diagrams or graphics. "A picture says a thousand words!".

Whilst setting up your proposal environment, you were asked to identify things that you do better than your competitors. If you are lucky, or if you manage to design your solution in this way, you can emphasise your great features.

You should also be able to find out what your clients will get excited about. We call these "Hot Spots". Ensure that your Hot Spots are very easy to find in your proposal.

As you become more experienced, you learn how to build in upgrades into your proposal. These are items that you think that you can sell over and above what is in the proposal. Many large companies do this very profitably and it is a lesson that you should learn as quickly as possible. Subtly is the way to do it – no one wants to read a heavy sales fest! Make sure that you are separating them from your proposal so that there is no question as to what is included within your proposal.

Hiding The Saggy Bits

Now your problem areas – just as you can dress to hide your saggy bits – you can design your proposal to hide the bits you are not strong on – on even can't do. First of all position them, if you can in the middle of the left hand part of the page. This is the least looked at part of a proposal. Also surround them with Hot Spots so that better things are remembered.

If you have stuff that you really can't do – this is where those wonderful things called caveats come in. Basically caveats say "….we can't do that, but we can do this, which is much better…." So if a piece of equipment does not meet their specifications but is better in other areas, you say something like this. "Our widgets do not osserfact, however we have designed them to be produce a better performance by delleticing!"

Writing caveats that are truthful, but still make your products and services look great is something that you need to practice. It will be worth it.

Writing The Proposal

Now its time to get down to actually writing the proposal. ITT's come in several different formats, and hopefully they all come with instructions as to how your potential client wants the proposal to look like. The usual formats are:

Service or Goods Required ITT's

This is the easiest proposal. Examples of this might be to provide 100 widgets; Paint the outside of a house; provide security services for a car park etc.

You should start by introducing your company, then describe your goods or services, ensuring that you meet the client's need. Then identify your superiority or USP and why you would be the best company. Lastly include an up beat closing statement.

List ITT's

In this kind of ITT you will be provided with a list of items required. This is more common with the supplier of goods ITT. Winning this kind of proposal is often won by price, but you need to also establish the quality of your goods as well as the promptness and reliability of your delivery and support.

Question and Answer ITT's

Often you will get an ITT that is a list of questions – all requiring answers. You need to be careful that you include your USP and branding in the answers. You will probably get questions on your company – which is where you blow you trumpet about how great you are. Great care should be taken with your cover letter so that you fan provide a winning overview of your proposal.

Solution Based ITT's

As you get to bigger ITT's, they will often give you a request or a problem and ask you for the solution.   This is very common in the IT and business solution and services environment. These are the most complex to answer but they do allow you the liberty of promoting your business and solution as being the best.

There is an old mantra in report writing: "Tell them what you are going to say. Tell them. Tell them why you told them.   It means: introduce your proposal, define the proposal and then summarise the best bits that you have written.

Complex ITT's

These are a combination of the above two ITT's. You will be presented with the situation as it is at the moment and then a picture of where your potential client wishes their business to be. In addition they will often separate the ITT into sections such as goods, services, support, training etc and ask you questions on each. They may also ask you to identify your proposal for each section.

Putting It All Together

You can also win or lose a proposal on your presentation. In the last chapter we discussed where to place your great and saggy bits. Here we look at what your proposal looks like as well as the words you use.

Why is the presentation of your bid so important?

- It takes you from Wish to Win.
- Presents your good points and hides your weaknesses.
- Keeps the evaluator's attention.
- Ensures that your proposal is remembers when the evaluation is undertaken.

The Proposal Structure

In order to produce a winning proposal your must consider:

- Who the bid is for
- What they are really looking for
- How to present yourself in the best manner

Who are your audience? You may be lucky and get only one or two evaluators, but each part of your proposal will evaluated in the following way. In a larger proposal, you will have a group of evaluators who will have specific roles:

- **The deciders** – who will only look at executive summary and your pricing structure.
- **The business** – who will look at the non-technical explanations to meet their expectations and needs.
- **Technical reviewers** – who will want deep technical information.
- **Evaluators** – who will look at the supporting information and may wish to delve deeper.

Executive Summary

The executive summary is an important part of your proposal. The real deciders will not be reading the entire bid – they will rely on their technical reviewers, but the executive summary should sell to them in easy to understand descriptions.

In a smaller proposal the executive summary sets out and summarises your entire proposal.

It can be used to emphasise your strengths and explain why you are the best company to do the project. It is often the first and last thing to be read and tends to stick in the mind so you must spend a lot of time and effort on it. Don't rush it.

Conclusion

The last thing they read in your proposal so it will be the last thought on your bid. It should include:

- Your thanks for the opportunity to bid – good manners are always remembered.
- Summaries your strengths – take every opportunity to get these into the evaluator's memory.
- Details of the benefits of using your company.

- Other options that you can offer. This makes your company more attractive and could earn you some profit.
- The way forward. Always paint a picture of you both working together on the project. A bit like "walking into the sunset!".

Give your evaluators something to remember you by as they move onto the next bid to evaluate. If you are lucky, they will then be checking the other bid against yours to see how the others measure up.

Copyrights

A short note on copyrights, they are very important.

- Do not give yours away.
- Do not give other people's away.
- Define what will happen to new items.
- Do not make assumptions.

The Cover Letter

A short note on your cover letter: This should be used to present your proposal in its best light. It should be just under one page long, formally written and addressed to the key member of your potential client's evaluation team (found from the ITT). Do not forget to include you key selling points (subtly – this is a letter).

Other Bits and Bobs

Don't forget all of these things – they make your proposal much easier to navigate and understand.

- Table of contents
- Headers and footers –so that they know who's proposal they are reading and what page they are on.
- Confidentiality and copyright clauses – these are important to protect your business and appear professional.
- Covering letter – introduce yourself.

- Glossary of terms – especially in a technical arena but don't "talk down".
- Brochures – these can explain so much.
- Contact details – often forgotten but soooo important.
- CD/DVD copy. This helps with evaluating.

Do not forget

- All the odds and bobs that were also required.
- Your proposal should reflect your company's brand.
- Use standard templates, including your sub contractor's contribution.

In the heat of the moment – do not forget all the little things. I know of bids that have been lost because they were non compliant by forgetting something that was compulsory.

Presentation Golden Rules

P resentation is incredibly important and can help you win that bid. Good presentation makes you proposal easy to read and easy to understand. Remember:

- Follow any required presentation standards.
- Make your presentation reflect your brand and image.
- Keep your key information in the top $1/3^{rd}$ of the page.
- Use lots of white so that your pages are easy to read and the reader can easily find the appropriate information.
- Use graphics to explain and inform.
- Consistency, consistency, consistency!

To summarise, bid presentation is vital:

- **Hitting those hot spots** – By reading the ITT thoroughly as well as feed back from your sales people, you should know what your potential client's particular interests or "want to have's" are. Make sure that you address these hot spots, subtly but definitely in your proposal.

- **Graphics and text** – It is true a picture does paint a thousand words. Bids can be technical and somewhat boring and are not always read by technical people. Use a graphic or picture to show part of the solution/service and then explain it underneath.

- **Making your point** – Clarity and succinctness in a proposal is a good indicator of the quality of the products and services that may be produced. Will you client want a project that rambles on and on and never seems to conclude?

- **Easy on the eye** – As an experienced evaluator who reads multiple bids on the same subject, I can tell you that a proposal that reads well and is comfortable to read is a blessing and always well remembered.

- **Subtly offering extra services** - The key word is subtle. Indicate within your bid that you are offering what your client wants, but can offer so much more that they may require in the future. Your client may think that best company to start a relationship with is the one that they can grow with.

Proposal Writing For Smaller Businesses
Who Want To Become Bigger Businesses!

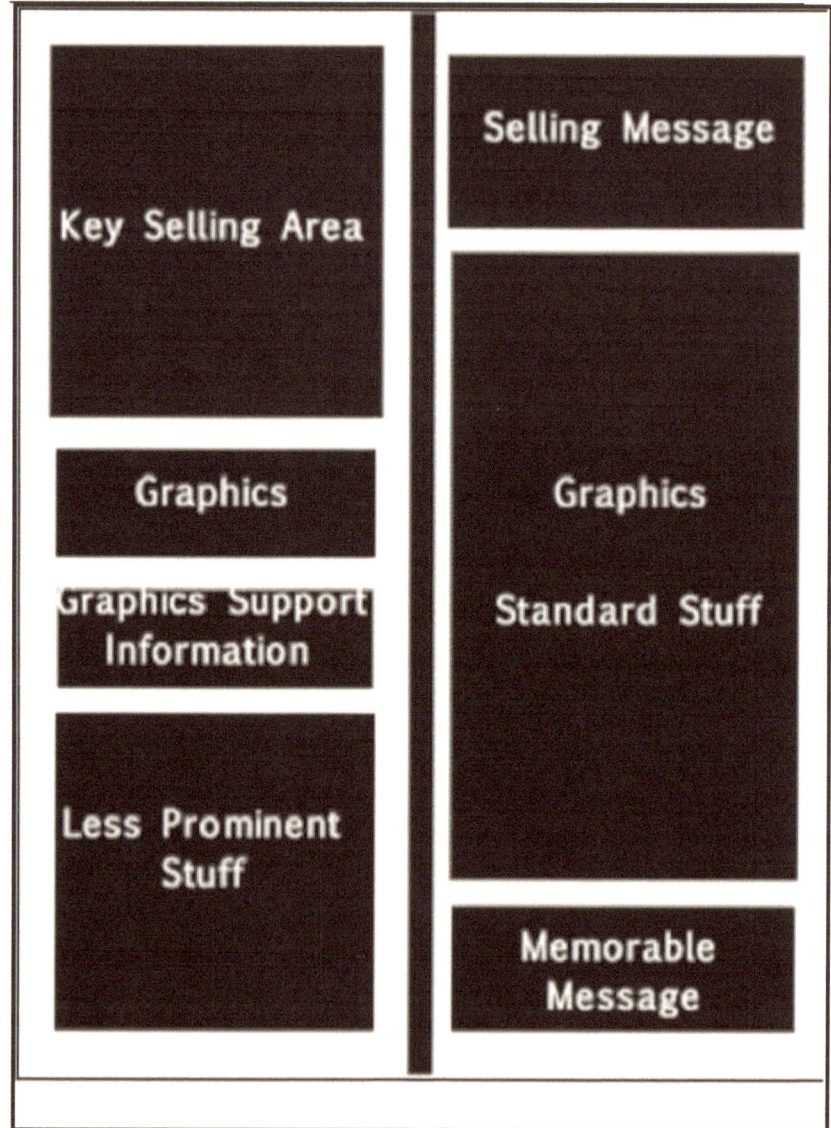

Making Yourself Look Bigger

Your business brand says a lot about you and your business. If you create a strong brand image, it will elevate you above your peers and provide a good model for your product and service development as well as a sound foundation from which to expand your business.

So what is Branding?

Many people think that having a logo and maybe a short description of their services is all they need to set up their brand. This is not so. Your brand encompasses all that your business does, from first contact with your potential customers through to how your products are defined and sold.

Your brand is what defines and describes your business. Look at any two different companies that compete in the same market and look at how people recognize and remember them.

Using good branding makes your business seem more successful, established and somewhat bigger.

When writing your proposal it is important that it is consistent, memorable and recognisable as your company. This means that it should use one font – the same that your company uses. At Biz Guru Ltd, for example we always use Verdana because it is open, clear and easy to understand.

Every part of your proposal should include your company name and logo. You can easily do this by putting them on the header and footer of all your documents. All your marketing materials that you include in your proposal should have the same look and feel as well as the same design structure.

Lastly to make your company more memorable you should have a Unique Selling Point (USP).

Your Unique Selling Point

Often called the U.S.P – it means – "What makes your company, product and services different from all the other companies selling the same thing?

Now obviously in a crowded business environment – be it click or brick – you want your company to not only stand out but be memorable.

So how do I define my U.S.P.?

Have a look at you company and a few companies that you believe compete with you. Also look at a couple of companies who are trading as you would wish to trade in the next few years. For products we mean products, goods or services.

So, what product features could you have that would make you different from your competitors?

- Look at what products you sell the most often or most of.
- How do these products differ from each other?
- What benefits do these products provide?
- What better features do you/ you could provide?
- What features do competitor's products have that yours do not. What features do your products have that are different you're your competitors?

Make yourself stand out from your competitors and emphasise this in all your fully branded proposals and you should not only be noticeable above others but also look larger, more professional and memorable. What more do you want?

Differentiating Your Company From Others

You are now hard at work writing your tender or proposal in the hope of winning that big new contract, but you know that you have at least one, if not more, big competitor. You'd like to differentiate your company and make it seem much better than them. You've also got some great products that are better than their as well. So how do you do this and win that great bid?

Well first of all look at your business and then specifically at the products and services that you are offering. You then need to look at your prices, fulfilment and support. Lastly look at the staff that will be working on the project and supporting the new service or system. Here are a few questions to ask yourself in order for you to list how much greater your business and bid is than all the others?

Look at your business compared to theirs?

- Is your business larger or more dominant than your competitor's?

- Are your products better, more well-known or better marketed than your competitor's?

- Have you been in business longer and are more established?

- Is your brand image more prominent or has a better reputation?

- Are you more local to your potential customer?

- Are your prices and price break points better than theirs?

- Do you offer a better range of payment methods or option?

- Do you offer better payment discounts than they do?

- Do you fulfil orders quicker than they do?

- Do you have better incentives than they do?

- Do you have better products and product ranges than they do?

- Do you have better customer, maintenance and sales support?
- Is your fulfilment faster or better than the competitor's?
- Do you install or build things faster?
- Do you have "first to the market" or latest technology advantage?

Look at your services, product and staff.

- Identify the features you have that they don't have. What features are better in yours?
- What statistics do you have on your product that you can use to show your uniqueness or superiority?
- What physical or emotional needs/desires/requirements does your product meet that theirs does not?
- Is your product more up to date, modern or technically advanced?
- Does your product last longer than the competitor's?

- Are your products; bigger, smaller, faster, slower, more robust, higher etc?

- Are your staff more highly trained or do you have one or more subject experts?

- What type of customer support are you going to offer and how does it differ from your competitor?

- Do you offer a special type of professional advice or support that they don't? If so, what?

- How is your confidentiality different than your competitors?

Once you've worked through these you should be able to write some great paragraphs showing how great your business, staff and products are. If you can't write great prose – then be brave and bullet point your great points.

Pricing To Win

Pricing is often the win or lose activity in your proposal and great care should be taken on the arrival on your final price. Don't leave it to the last minute!

There are several ways to calculate the work required in a project.

- On a daily, weekly or monthly basis so that the work in undertaken in a methodical manner such that larger individual jobs are regularly attended to.
- On a time and material manner for one off or regular jobs.

Estimate how long it will take one or more members of your staff to do the work. Take your hourly staff rate, add extra for any special materials you need. Add your profit and you have your cost. For a regular account your profit level should be lower. You could also offer a lower "introductory" fee for so that they can test out the new company.

The Pricing Model

A Pricing Model should be produced in the format requested in the ITT. It should take into account any NPV calculations that are required. Care should be taken to ensure that the correct level of detail is provided. No more and no less as don't want to give away any more costing information than you need to. Don't forget to build in some return for the risks that you will undertake,

You should be careful that you split out taxes (VAT or as appropriate to your country) and handle delivery charge as specified in the ITT. Sometimes bids can be provide on a "time and material basis" – in which case you need to place a floor and ceiling on your costs and specify exactly what time and the materials are.

Teasers, that is, other services that can be supplied for an extra cost can also be included - although care should be taken to stipulate that these are extras!

Managing The Risky Bits

Risk costs money and can be what makes your project fail! So it makes sense to be able to recognise and mitigate it. This chapter is a little complex but it will save you money so please read it.

A risk is an event that is likely to cause an adverse impact to one or more of the following:

- **Project budget** – what it is going to cost you to implement the winning solution.
- **Project timeline** – how long it will REALLY take.
- **Project deliverables** – what you have contracted to produce.
- **Project resources** – what you will need to get to full implementation.

If you win the proposal and undertake the project.

You need to examine your attitude to risk:

- What level of risk is acceptable?
- What kinds of risks are acceptable?
- How do you cost the risks you accept?

Managing bid risk consists of three activities:

- Identifying risk.
- Measuring risk.
- Mitigating risk.

Identifying Risks

Risks fall into the following categories:

- **Contractual** - in the contract but also invitation to tender (ITT).
- **Financial** - your pricing model or that imposed upon you.
- **Project** – how you undertake and complete the project. Will the project work?
- **Internal** – how you business and staff work and what kind of resources you have available.

Proposal Writing For Smaller Businesses
Who Want To Become Bigger Businesses!

Go through the contract, payment schedule and your proposed approach to the project and identify each risk that you come across. This is best done on a spreadsheet or similar.

Measuring Risk

Once you have identified each risk. You need to put a number between 1-10 against each risk, to identify how likely the risk is to happen. Then in the next column, put a number between 1 -5 to highlight the impact of the risk. If you multiply these two numbers together you will get some idea of how much you need to worry about the risk. If you are more comfortable you can set yourself a numerical level for low, medium and high risk.

Risk	Likelihood	Impact	Total
Risk 1 (High)	7	5	35
Risk 2 (Low)	1	3	3
Risk 3 (Medium)	4	2	14

Mitigating Risk

Here is where you use your caveats that we discussed in a previous chapter. There are three ways that you can deal with risk:

- Accept it so no comments are required.
- Accept it with caveats.
- Refuse to accept it and give polite reasons why not.

Being A Small Fish In A Big Pond

As mentioned before, it is sometimes prudent to work with other companies when bidding on a larger project. This will enable you to stretch your company and learn new skills as well as put your company's name amongst "the big boys".

Working with others does come with its own problems though – not least of which is each party's responsibilities and remunerations. It is absolutely imperative that you have a contract with each other that:

- Reflects the contract with your client – i.e. it trickles down and each clause in the main contract is on the individual contracts.
- Identifies each company's responsibilities, deliverables, payment schedules, managing staff and who is the boss and when.
- Is agreeable to both parties.
- Ensures that each business is only responsible for matters that is has some influence over!

Asking Those Pertinent Questions

Sometimes during the proposal writing period you will get an opportunity to ask your potential clients questions. In a formal situation your competitors will also get the same opportunity and these question and answer periods are often held with you all together. You therefore need to ensure that the questions you ask do not give any clues as to your strengths or weaknesses to your competitors.

When asking your questions you need to ensure that:

- Your questions are relevant and pertinent.
- You do not put doubts as to your abilities to successfully complete the project into your potential client's minds.
- You do not give any advantages to your rivals e.g. by asking questions that allow them to show their strengths.

Ensure that you take note of the answers!

So What Could Possibly Go Wrong?

So what can possibly go wrong with your proposal?

Missing The Deadline

It's late, everyone is tired, the deadline is looming and the proposal is in pieces all over the place. There must be an easier way? Well if you have a complex proposal how about a Plan? Your plan will have:

- Who's writing which bit of the proposal
- Where it goes in the proposal.
- When it needs to be completed by.

Getting The Costs and Pricing Wrong

Double check your costs and you should ensure that:

- The pricing is in correct format as per the ITT. You do not have to make all your calculations common knowledge.
- Taxes and delivery are accounted for.

Missing Out Vital Bits

At the start of the proposal writing process you should make a list of all bits you want to put into the proposal and tick them off as you put them into your proposal. Bits usually missed off are the brochures, standard documents and the signature on the end of the proposal.

Incorrect Solution

The best prepared proposal still will not make a profit if the solution is incorrect, so here is a check list of things that can go wrong in a project. Try not to let it depress you too much.

1. Poor analysis or visualisation of current needs.
2. Pre-conceived ideas as to the solution.
3. Unreasonable expectations of the budget and resources needed.
4. Unreasonable expectations from client or users.
5. Lack of support and/or interest.
6. Risks, costs and benefits incorrectly measured.
7. Poor project management.
8. Inappropriate project management methods.

9. Lack of controls.

10. Poor communication.

11. Quality not measured or controlled.

12. Poorly developed systems or processes.

13. Poor planning mechanisms.

14. Inappropriate or ineffective organisational structures.

15. Low confidence on in-house computer group.

16. Inappropriate mix of skills in project team.

17. Lack of training and formal skills.

18. Low confidence in the project team.

19. Loss of project momentum.

20. Resistance to change "WE'VE ALWAYS DONE IT THIS WAY".

21. Suspicion or conflict.

22. Inadequate analysis or testing.

23. Poor technology transfer.

24. Poor documentation.

25. Poor or inappropriate training.

Good project management will solve most of them – but that's another of my books!

Well.... You Won!

Congratulations you won – so off you go and get that project started. Good luck. Let's work out what you have learnt from this process.

- Prepare for every bid – preparation helps you win bids.
- Organise yourself for ease and speed.
- Understand your potential client's needs.
- Review what you did right and wrong and learn from them.
- Record what you plan to do and what you did and do the right things again.
- Reuse as much as possible in your next bid.

Final Thought

> **When you are up to your ears in crocodiles it is difficult to remember that your original intent was to drain the swamp.**

Proposal Writing For Smaller Businesses
Who Want To Become Bigger Businesses!

Index

Proposal Writing For Smaller Businesses
Who Want To Become Bigger Businesses!

Proposal Writing For Smaller Businesses
Who Want To Become Bigger Businesses!

www.ingramcontent.com/pod-product-compliance
Lightning Source LLC
Chambersburg PA
CBHW030903180526
45163CB00004B/1681